HAPPINESS

In 30 Days Or Less

By

Marc Royer Ph.D.

Happiness in 30 Days Or Less

Copyright 1998
The Christian Resource Group
First Printing 1998

Scripture quotations are taken from
New International Version
Copyright 1983, Zondervan Corporation
Used by permission

All rights reserved. No part of this book may be produced in any form. Except for the inclusion of brief quotations in a review or article, without Written permission from the author or publisher.

Published by:
The Christian Resource Group
11664 Red Oak Dr.
Granger, Indiana 46530
(219) 273-6235

ISBN: 1-57502-816-6
Library of Congress Catalog Card Number: 98-91486

Printed in the USA by

MORRIS PUBLISHING

3212 East Highway 30 • Kearney, NE 68847 • 1-800-650-7888

TABLE OF CONTENTS
"Happiness in 30 Days Or Less"

Introduction	4
Day 1: Slow Down	5
Day 2: Enjoy the Moment	10
Day 3: Adjust Your Attitude	13
Day 4: Forgive Someone	17
Day 5: Give Something Away	20
Day 6: Put Others First	23
Day 7: Count Your Blessings	26
Day 8: Stay Pleasant	29
Day 9: Downsize	32
Day 10: Lower Your Debt	35
Day 11: Simplify Your Systems	38
Day 12: Eat Less	41
Day 13: Look For the Best	44
Day 14: Get Rid Of Guilt	47
Day 15: Cherish Others	49
Day 16: Save Some Money	52
Day 17: Drink Water	55
Day 18: Notice Little Things	58
Day 19: Waste Some Time	61
Day 20: Chill Out	64
Day 21: Face Your Fear	67
Day 22: Clip Your Credit Cards	70
Day 23: Manage Your Anger	73
Day 24: Admit to Weaknesses	76
Day 25: Think Only Positive	78
Day 26: Live On/With Less	81
Day 27: Always Be Kind	84
Day 28: Let Go	86
Day 29: Take A Step Back	89
Day 30: Let Yourself Be Happy	92

INTRODUCTION

Are you looking for happiness? Most of us are. Where do you look for it? Happiness is one of the most elusive things in the world. Just when you think you have hold of it -- there it goes, slipping away again.

How would you respond if you were told that you were trying too hard? Further that the happiness that has eluded you is not just at your fingertips, but is within you. Because happiness is already inside of you, all you really need are the tools to bring it out. Of the 30 ideas described in this book, all you need is to start applying a couple of them before you see this truth revealed. After trying a couple of these ideas, you will then see how, as you apply more of them, happiness will be multiplied to you. Just when you think you are as happy as any one could be, you will go into deeper levels. Your new life will be contagious. It will change your whole world. Your home, your family, your work, your relationships, your future --everything will begin to change as you apply these ideas to your life.

As you work through all 30 ideas, you will find some harder and some easier for you personally. Apply what you can of each point. Allow the rest to stay with you through time. Don't rush it. You have spent most of your life the way you are -- changing is going to take some time. But it should be fun. Reading and applying these 30 principles should give you plenty to work on, but also plenty of satisfaction. Everything you need is within you. These principles were created to jump-start your happiness batteries. Get that charge up in those batteries and have fun doing it!

DAY 1: SLOW DOWN

Very few of us would deny a need to slow down. The reason we don't varies from person to person, but the bottom line is -- we think if we slow down we will miss out on something. Further, we are conditioned early on in life that if we would only work harder, faster, or longer, success will be our benefactor.

Everything is speeding up. It can be seen in what psychologists are beginning to research in driving habits. The speed of our day is projected in our driving. Professionals, who are studying this, call it "driving rage." The frustration, pressure, and stress of the day are coming out in how we deal with other cars in traffic. There are more and more cars on the road, more accidents, and more serious injury than ever before. The seriousness of any accident is in direct proportion to the speed of the vehicle. Speed equals injury. Slow down.

Career endeavor has much to do with speed. Regardless of what vocation is yours, the "fast track" is often the goal. This speedy course requires office politics, mind games, manipulation, image enhancement, nights out, weeks away, and the constant need to please someone else. What we don't stop to realize is this "fast track" is a treacherous course. You can achieve all your career goals, but at the same time ignore, deny, and lose those things you once held dear. If you achieve career success but lose your family, your wife, your life, and even your own soul -- what have you really achieved? You may have won the game, but lost the war. You may win the whole world, have everything you always wanted, but miss out on happiness.

Slow down. Another thing could happen to you that is equally devastating. This scenario is happening more and more. You could give your soul to your career and be "downsized" with your corporation. Many casualties have been left in the wake of decisions from those who have already "made it." The employees did everything they could to prove themselves only to find it was not enough. In the process they became alienated from their families, divorced, broke, lonely, and without the career they sacrificed it all for. Slow down.

Family life speeds up. Everybody has his or her own interests and even different world each travel in. Everyone's schedule speeds up because of the expectation each feels to please others outside of the family and the need to be accepted in the world they live. Families today spend very little time together at all. The only time most families spend together is in a rush; rushing to this game or to that one -- or spreading time between two games occurring at the same time. Dinner is brought home from a drive-through fast food joint. The family is on a crash and burn course and doesn't even realize it because everyone they know leads just as hectic of a life. Families need to slow down.

Check out the channels at any time of the day or night on your local cable system. Advertising is geared toward getting rich quick, crash diets, predicting your future by a telephone call to a psychic, toll free numbers, charge it, and rush delivery. All of these things are speeding up our expectations, our attitudes, and our lives.

How does it happen -- slowing down and finding happiness? It is much easier than you might imagine. Happiness is within you. The reason many people are not happy is because they are in too big of a rush. The speed of life causes happiness to become suppressed. Life falls into a rut of running around doing a bunch of things rather than taking the time to "be." Whenever we fall into the trap of "doing" rather than "being," the only way to rectify the situation is to slow down.

The first step in slowing down and becoming happier in your life is to become more conscious of the need to slow down. If you want to seriously apply this idea there is an exercise you can do. Make a decision that for a period of one month you will obey every traffic law down to the precise detail. You will come to complete stops, take your turn at four ways, not pass on the right side shoulder, and most importantly -- drive the posted speed limit. What makes this exercise effective is that you will become more conscious of just how often people disregard traffic laws. This disregard is often the reason for so many accidents. If you follow through on this commitment, you will be amazed at how conscious you will become of how others drive. You won't be able to disregard your own behavior. The result will be an amazing projection of this lesson on to other areas of your life.

The second step in slowing down and becoming happier in your life is to slow down by slowing up. Slowing down does not mean your life should come to a complete stop! It wouldn't be practical for anyone to bring his life to a screeching halt to change a direction. Those who have tried this approach usually end up with disastrous results. Slowing down your life is a process. You can be a success in this process if you start with slowing up. Start by discarding those things you don't need to be doing. Constantly ask yourself: Why am I doing this? (And) Is this something I have to do? These questions are not an end, but a beginning to start thinning out your schedule.

Slowing up means that you start with yourself. It is a common mistake to start slowing up those around you while leaving yourself out of the slowing down "loop." If you expect those around you to be the ones slowing down, and you leave yourself out, you will create great resentment in others. The end will be worse than the beginning. Take responsibility for slowing up areas of your life.

The third step in slowing down and becoming happier in your life is to practice "slow down moments" several times per day. When you find yourself getting caught up in the rush of the day -- take a break from the rush. This will take things a step further than just being conscious of the rush. Whether it is rushing the kids to soccer practice, music lessons, parent meetings, or clubs, taking "slow down moments" will force you to ask yourself -- How necessary is this activity? This is something that can be done with your family, friends, and fellow employees present. Actually, the more people present when you take a "slow down moment," the better. When others in your life become aware of the pace of life and how lives intersect and cause things to speed up, the "slow down moment" becomes penetrating.

The fourth step in slowing down and becoming happier in your life is to take an occasional "mental break." A mental break can take many different forms during the course of a day. Whether it is a cup of coffee or a television program, these breaks are an essential part of slowing you down. Taking mental breaks will actually prevent a mental breakdown. The reason many people don't take a break is to avoid guilt. Feelings of guilt go much deeper emotionally than can be solved by a break, but it is a start in learning that happiness is within you.

Don't just take a break every few hours -- enjoy the break you are taking. Don't take the same break, the same way each time, or your break can actually cause you stress. This kind of stress comes from a feeling of expectation from ruts we create. Change your breaks. Take some breaks with others. Take some by yourself. Let some breaks include food. Let some breaks be wacky. Some breaks should cause you to sweat and breathe hard. Others should be as easy as a nap. People who don't take a break are not happy people. Be happy...take a break!

YOU CAN BECOME
HAPPY BY SLOWING
DOWN:

1. Become more conscious of how you rush around.

2. Slow yourself up.

3. Take a "slow down moment."

4. Take a mental break.

DAY 2: ENJOY THE MOMENT

Picture the life that would make you happy. Put it together in your mind. Add some detail to this happy life. What is the first thing you pictured? There is significance in how you put this picture together. The picture we put together of happiness often relates to a future event. The problem is that future event never gets here.

We have today. Today is comprised of 24 hours with 60 minutes in each hour. Those happy thoughts of some kind of future event needs to be brought into the now...today. Happiness comes a minute at a time. Enjoy the moment.

Throughout your day there are defining moments. These are happy moments if we choose to enjoy them as such. The reason we don't enjoy the moments the way we should is because we don't take the time to. They happen quickly and slip away. A happy thought, a comment, a laugh, enjoyment, pleasure, beautiful scenery or conversation will slip by virtually unnoticed, unless we take the time to enjoy it. Enjoy the moment.

Enjoying the moment and becoming happy in your life requires you to look for a happy moment. If you are looking for a moment to enjoy, you will find it. This needs to be a priority every day of your life. Whether you are working or not, weekend or weekday, vacation or business always look for a happy moment.

Once you begin to notice these moments, enjoying them can be a different matter. Enjoying the moment and becoming happy in your life requires you to take the time to enjoy the moment. Letting a moment linger requires plenty of discipline, especially if you are used to passing right past those special moments. You can also feel down right inconvenienced if you are not used to enjoying a moment.

Enjoying the moment happens naturally. Let yourself laugh. If you laugh, let it go on a little longer. Look a little harder, a little longer, and a little more often at those things you would normally be taking for granted. Enjoying the moment and becoming happy in life requires you to not take things for granted.

You might think that you are trying your best to live the best life you can. If that is how you see yourself, you will probably be a little offended by the suggestion that you might be taking things for granted in your life. Offended or not, all of us take too many things for granted. Taking things for granted makes many of us unhappy with our lives.

If we discipline ourselves to begin to enjoy the moment more, it will mean we will be taking things for granted less. The inverse is also true -- if we take definite steps to not take things for granted we will free ourselves up to enjoy more moments of our lives.

Learning to enjoy the moment is a major step toward a brand new life. The more moments you learn to enjoy the more total enjoyment you will have with every moment of your life.

Remember that our lives are simply a chain of moments. The longer we linger, the longer the period of time will be. While learning to enjoy the moment, you will actually condition yourself to enjoy your life. This new enjoyment will truly bring the happiness to your life you desire.

Squeeze the most out of every moment and you will be able to squeeze the most out of every day -- and you will feel happy about doing it. Workaholics work in an attempt to achieve something they cannot define, and accomplish goals that leave them empty. As much as they work, workaholics are addicted to a feeling of worth, which comes from a deep sense of no self worth. Further, workaholics have no ability within their frame of mind to enjoy the moment. Workaholics are not happy people, not because they don't want to be happy, they just don't know how. Here is how: Enjoy the moment.

ENJOYING THE MOMENT
AND BECOMING HAPPY
REQUIRES:

1. Looking for a happy moment.

2. Taking time to enjoy the moment.

3. Not taking the moments of life for granted.

DAY 3: ADJUST YOUR ATTITUDE

Feelings are fickle. If your car breaks down on the way to work, the way you feel is affected. You feel lousy, hassled, and even victimized. Depending upon how you personally react to being inconvenienced, you can experience various degrees of anxiety and panic. On the other side, once your car is fixed, you feel relieved. The relief of your car being fixed can cause a great swing of emotion. The only way to control emotional swings of how you feel is to be able to adjust your own attitude.

Getting control of one's life is the goal of many. The reason this goal is elusive is because so many things in life are out of our control. Just spend some time living, and you will find out quickly that things don't always turn out the way you want them to. Dreams shatter, goals go unachieved, and even disaster may strike. Sometimes people feels trapped, or out of control, or both at the same time.

We all have the need to be in control of something. This need comes from the deepest levels within us. We must be able to control something so that we can change or enhance the direction of our lives. There is something we can control -- it is our own attitude. Your whole world is based upon your own attitude. If you can adjust your attitude you have the power to adjust your whole world.

Adjusting your own attitude will bring happiness in your life because it changes how you view life. It is not what physically happens in your world that affects your life, it is how you see and interpret (your perception) of things in your life. Your perception is all attitudes. If you perceive something that just happened as negative, it will be negative. But, if you perceive that same thing as positive, it will be positive. How something affects you is completely up to you. You have control over the effect. It all occurs through your attitude. You may or may not have any control over an outcome, but you do have the entire control over your perception of an outcome. Adjust your attitude and you will see this happen before your eyes!

Adjusting your own attitude will bring happiness in your life because it will change your entire world. If you adjust your attitude, life as you know it will change forever. People will be attracted to you because they will know you have something in your life that they long to have. They won't even know what it is, but they will know they need it. That one thing that brings happiness is adjusting your attitude.

Adjusting your attitude will so alter how you see things that you won't believe the possibilities and opportunities you have created for yourself. Adjusting your attitude will be like taking off blinders that you have had on your entire life.

Adjusting your own attitude will bring happiness in your life because you will see a flow and cadence in living which brings you success. Adjusting your attitude involves no one else but you. Looking at things positively rather than negatively will create a force of flow so strong in your life that you will live the life you always desired. Everything you always wanted will flow into your life because you will see it and acknowledge it. This flow might already be happening, but because we allow our feelings to rule us, we don't (or can't) see it. If your perception won't allow you to see positive blessings occurring in your life, it will be as though the flow is not happening at all. If you never acknowledge the positive flow in your life, the flow will shrink up.

You can adjust your attitude by simply choosing to do so. When those negative feelings creep in, remind yourself to change your attitude and look at things differently. Don't get sucked into those negative feelings, which begin a downward spiral into despair. If you are prone to looking at things through the lens of the worst possible scenarios -- train yourself not to do that. The worst things are not going to happen to you! It is often said that 95% of the things we spend time worrying about don't come to pass. If this were true, it would mean we spend most of our lives worrying about things which won't occur anyway.

Negative emotions have a way of robbing us of happiness, which is ours to enjoy. At this point each of us is our own worst enemy (or greatest help).

Adjusting your attitude is no respecter of persons. People often think they are too old to change. It doesn't matter how young or old you are, you can change. The change can start right now, this moment. All you need to do is start adjusting your attitude throughout the day. It is easier than you think. Why put it off?

If you need some help in getting attitude adjustment started in your life, try to remember two things. First, whatever is happening in your life, it is happening for a reason. Let that reason always be to help teach you something. Teachable people are happy people. They are always learning something from the circumstances around them. Secondly, always remember that everything passes. Life is based upon cycles. Remember the old adage, "this too will pass." If you remember this, the circumstances won't seem so final.

ADJUSTING YOUR OWN ATTITUDE WILL BRING HAPPINESS IN YOUR LIFE BECAUSE:

1. It changes how you see things.

2. It changes your entire world.

3. You will experience a flow and cadence in life, which brings you success.

DAY 4: FORGIVE SOMEONE

If you are holding something against someone it will be impossible to be happy. The reason is simple: the same emotion that allows you to be happy is used to be angry with someone. In this way, unhappiness and anger displace your happiness. The good news is -- it is within your own power to change it!

If you made it through the last paragraph, you are dying to call me up and tell me all the dynamics around the situation with the person you are mad at. The truth is: You have every reason to be mad, hurt, upset, and angry. When you talk about it to others, they will agree with you. No one you talk to about the dynamics of a situation in which you were hurt will disagree with you. It is just easier to agree with you because no one can help you but you.

There is something that goes deeper than just explaining your situation to others and gaining empathy. Empathy will only go so far. No matter how many others agree with you, hurt with you, or reach out to you, it will not bring you happiness. Happiness will only come when you decide to forgive someone! Learning how to forgive someone is really a simple process involving a decision rather than unpredictable passion.

Step #1: Realize that carrying something against someone is getting old. When you are carrying something against someone, it will emerge from you all the time. Your friends will begin to avoid you, but you will not even realize it. Your relationships will become shaky. You won't realize what is happening. The hurt you are carrying is causing it, but because you are so caught up in hurt, you will not even see the lack of forgiveness in your own life as the cause.

Step #2: Realize that no one can do anything about this situation but you. This is the most important step. People who have been hurt often lose their balance in life. When you lose your balance, your own center is missing. Even if every person on the planet agreed with you that someone else did you wrong not a single one of them can do anything to resolve the issue. Some people try sending messages back and forth through other people. Anyone who has ever tried triangulating others realizes it only makes matters worse.

Step #3: Realize that your only option is to forgive. There is no set resolve to hurtful situations. Many times people are dead before resolve is even considered. It is also true that reconciliation will never happen without forgiveness. Forgiveness is like the door that has to be opened before happiness can be restored to a life.

Step #4: Realize that forgiveness is simply a decision. Forgiveness is an act of the will. You choose to forgive. This step becomes easier as you learn to forgive. At first it seems easier not to forgive, but after realizing it gets old, and no one else can help you but you, making the decision to forgive will make the most sense.

Shortly after forgiving, you will experience a kind of rush that has been missing for some time. That rush is actually the happiness you have been missing while you were mad at someone or something.

In the process of forgiveness don't overlook a key issue -- forgiveness is not complete until you forgive yourself. Most of the time we are too busy blaming others that we don't want to face up to the deeply felt need to forgive ourselves. The lack of self-forgiveness is why people become defensive and self absorbed. In an attempt to deal with issues, people find it easier to blame and deny, than to accept responsibility and move on. Life is too short to be robbed of the quality of happiness, which can be yours if you would simply learn to forgive yourself.

RECOVERING YOUR
HAPPINESS BY LEARNING
TO FORGIVE REQUIRES
ME TO REALIZE:

1. It is getting old being mad.

2. No one can do anything about this but me.

3. My only option is forgiveness.

4. Forgiveness is a decision.

DAY 5: GIVE SOMETHING AWAY

People rarely achieve happiness because they are always looking for that one special thing not yet achieved which will usher them into a state of ecstasy. The reason most accomplishments in life seem anticlimactic is because events don't provide long term happiness.

Many are looking for happiness in a material way. Because true happiness is internal, nothing external or material can give you any sense of lasting happiness. This is illustrated by children at Christmas. The anticipation of opening presents is generally the greater excitement than the actuality of opening them. There is joy in embracing a gift, but every gift eventually gets old. Every material thing has a relatively short shelf life compared to our emotional attachment to its potential for happiness to our lives.

There is something along these lines which causes us to become disillusioned when trying to find happiness: the more we get, the more we realize that happiness is not going to come by getting. Disillusionment sets in because soon we discover that happiness will never come this way. Happiness never occurs naturally. Just the opposite is true: happiness does not come by getting, but by giving. In this way less is always more.

If you want to achieve happiness, you have to be a giver, not a getter. Life does not condition us to be a giver. That is why it will take some work. We are conditioned to get--go after it--push--pull--take--make it work for you. Gaining happiness in life through becoming a giver requires changing up the way you think about things. It always requires you to develop a plan to implement, which has giving as its goal. This plan will help to recondition your life to be a giver, not a getter.

The first thing to do is to start listening to the needs of others. Most of the time we spend our energy on thinking about what we don't have. Living life this way will prevent us from realizing there are others who have needs greater than our own. Don't offer opinions, advice or counsel. Just listen. The result of listening will give you a genuine empathy for others and a diminished feeling of what you think you need. If you internalize it properly, listening will help you see that you do have a happy life already.

Next, as you listen to the needs of others, ask yourself if you presently have what that person needs to succeed. It may be a ballpoint pen, a throw rug, an automobile, or money. The object is not the important part of this exercise -- the ability to internalize is. "One man's junk is another man's treasure" has never been truer than when you are dealing with what it takes to be happy. If you have what someone else needs to be successful, it should follow that you ask yourself: Why aren't I as successful as I want to be?

Thirdly, seriously consider giving this person the thing they need to succeed. The reason you should "consider" the idea and not run out and do it is because giving has to be heart felt. The need this person shares with you needs to check out. If you fall for someone's line who is trying to use you, it will create such great a suspicion that you won't help anyone again. Check it out. If the need is real, the result of your giving will last a lifetime. If it is a "con" job by someone, it will serve to cause you bitterness.

Fourth, don't put strings on your gift. Giving requires letting go and trusting someone else with the gift. If you attach strings on your gift, it will never reach its fulfillment of what it could do, nor will you achieve the happiness through giving that you desire. Let go of it. This letting go process is actually the greatest part of this exercise.

Finally, make every gift personal. Don't go out and buy a duplicate of something you have. Instead, give them what you have. The idea is to make the gift personal. Nothing will create the avenue for happiness like the feeling of giving for someone or something else.

YOU CAN ACHIEVE
HAPPINESS BY LEARNING
TO GIVE SOMETHING
AWAY USING THESE
STEPS:

1. Listen to what others need.

2. Ask yourself if you can help.

3. Consider giving them what they need.

4. Don't put strings on the gift.

5. Make the gift personal.

DAY 6: PUT OTHERS FIRST

The pursuit of happiness will seem unnatural to most people because an unspoken idea about happiness is that it is basically selfish. Further, because we think happiness is selfish, we are really not convinced it is something we should pursue. Due to this kind of mentality, the ways we pursue happiness are selfish ways. Happiness never really comes and we become frustrated.

Mentality like this can easily change as you realize happiness is not a selfish goal. More people are affected in a positive way through a person who has inner happiness, than a person who is not happy. The desire to be happy is not selfish; it is as natural as breathing. Anyone who draws breath has the desire and the right to be happy. Further, happiness is something others need. If others see you as a happy person, they will be attracted to you. They will want what you have to rub off on them. People basically mean well -- they just don't always know how to achieve those things they desire. If you are able to achieve happiness, all areas of your life will thrive because people will want what you have.

The change needed is simply to change up the way we pursue happiness. Many of these "change ups" have to do with wiping out selfishness, (which many of us realize we need to do). Putting others first is a great start in changing the selfish mentality which creeps into your life. The more selfish you have become, the harder putting others first will be. There are three practical places to start. Your ability to successfully apply putting others first in these areas will quickly put you on the road of happiness.

Put your family first. It is easy to be caught up in your own needs and wants. You spend your spare moments thinking about yourself. Often missed is that your family has some real needs as well. If you are serious about pursuing happiness in your life, you need to take the time to find out what the needs of your family are. It might be a new pair of gym shoes for one of the kids or more time with the spouse. Often, important needs get missed because you are not listening to family members. Begin to spend your spare moments thinking about how you are going to meet the needs of your family, and you will begin to feel the self-abandon feeling of happiness creeping into your life. Walk around in your children's rooms. Do it without complaining about the mess. Instead, look at their world. Their room is what their world is. It will show you what they like and what motivates them. It will also show you what their needs are. Meet their needs. Do it before you meet your own needs. Even if you think you are putting your family first, try this and see.

Put your work associates first. Whether you are an employee or an employer, this principle is an important one to apply when pursuing happiness. The work place is one of the most selfish environments that exist. Everyone looks out for himself or herself. Often there is not the "give" when it is necessary. Be the giver. It might not sound natural. It might even sound weak, but if you begin to put others first in the work place, you will see the whole place change before too long. The fear is that you will be taken advantage of. That might happen -- but then again -- it might show you a greater picture of what relationships in your life are really like. Rather than assume certain things of certain people, you will give them enough of an opening to really reveal themselves to you.

Let others go first. Whether you are rushing to be checked out at the grocery store or at a four way stop -- when in doubt -- let others go first. This will not feel natural, especially if you have spent your life rushing around trying to beat everyone else. Simple kindness is the greatest example of what love is. This kind of love needs to evidence itself in the simple things of life in which we all participate. Let others go first and you will be well on the way to better health, and inner happiness!

Putting others first requires you to mentally put others first. This is a step by step process which any of us can apply. Think about others first in the small things, and you will put others first in the big things. The happiness that will begin in your life will be enormous!

HAPPINESS WILL COME TO YOU IF YOU PUT OTHERS FIRST.

1. Put your family first: Meet their needs before buying your toys.

2. Put your work associates first.

3. Let others go first: In lines -- In traffic -- In life.

DAY 7: COUNT YOUR BLESSINGS

Happiness is a struggle for most people wanting to get the most out of their life. People with a drive for success or excellence usually are driven toward goal accomplishment or task completion. Goal and task oriented people generally lack the ability to thrive on relationships. They also have trouble finding satisfaction and fulfillment anywhere in their lives. They are not just unhappy, but often miserable, even though they are successful in everything they set their minds to do.

Happiness can also be a struggle for people who are more relationship oriented. These people often don't see enough progress in their relationships to feel very affirmed in themselves. This lack of affirmation is a general feeling of rejection, abuse, or lack of love. Relationship oriented people place too high of an expectation on a relationship and get disappointed by the result.

The answer to the struggle for happiness regardless of the type of person you are oriented toward is to begin to count your blessings.

When you count your blessings, it will change how you see things. Unhappiness is caused by looking at how you want things to be. Happiness is created by looking at things you already have. Remember that the happiness which has alluded you is already within you. In the same way, all you need to be happy, you already have. If you count your blessings, you will begin to see that you are already blessed. When you acknowledge that you are already blessed, you will open up your life to the multiplication of those blessings to your life.

Counting your blessings requires you to become an inventory taker. Taking a personal inventory means to name those people, situations, opportunities, and things which help you to live a positive life. The purpose of doing this occasionally is to realize this truth. The more often we take a positive inventory, the more readily we can pull ourselves out of the dol-drums which make us unhappy. After applying this point, you will begin to see your life in a different light. Instead of seeing all the things you miss out on, you will begin to see all the things you have at your disposal. It only takes counting your blessings a few times before it becomes a very important habit in your life that you will do all the time.

Counting your blessings requires you to retrain yourself to start thinking about what you are thankful for in your life. Training yourself to think differently requires a lot of work. People who are taking (retraining) seriously have ways to insure their success. For example, putting a quarter in a jar every time you begin to think negatively (and taking it out every time you think positively), is one way of reconditioning your behavior. Counting your blessings is a behavior which can be developed into a positive habit. Behaviors are acquired through conditioning and training. It is your choice to behave one way or behave another. There may be such a thing as a genetic propensity to behave one way or another, but even if you are genetically inclined to behave negatively, changing the behavior is possible. It requires the consistent application to change.

Counting your blessings requires you to look ahead to a bright and hopeful future. Anything you can do to think more positively about your life is important. When you count your blessings, your track record will reveal to you that you have a great future ahead. This thought will help surround your thinking with happiness. People will be attracted to you because they are thirsty for people who can help provide them with hope. Regardless of the kind of work you do for a living, counting your blessings will be a great benefit both for the present and the future.

Counting your blessings is the type of discipline that is life changing.

When you are counting your blessings it is important to mention your thankfulness out loud. Don't keep it to yourself. Make sure when you are expressing your thankfulness that you don't make it about you. If you do, it will seem to others like you are bragging. Counting your blessings is not about you at all, it is about others. When you are thankful for someone else let him or her know. Counting your blessings is never complete until someone else is blessed by it!

COUNTING YOUR
BLESSINGS REQUIRES
YOU:

1. To become an inventory taker.

2. To retrain your thinking into being thankful.

3. To look ahead to a bright and hopeful future.

DAY 8: STAY PLEASANT

Day to day reactions and responses often rob us of happiness. It is a repetitive cycle, which is hard to jump off because it involves our personal lives. The more often we respond harshly, negatively, or strongly, the more often it will be repeated. Our responses and reactions carry a model of conditioning which is much like letting the horse out of the barn by accident -- once out, it is very difficult to get the horse back in.

The situation becomes complicated because our responses and reactions also cause a great amount of guilt. The guilt adds to the load of negative responses, which multiplies unhappiness. Defensiveness begets more defensiveness. The fear of rejection causes us to keep our masks firmly in place. Our image becomes more important than anything else does because fear of what others might think of us controls our lives.

Somewhere along the way we have to realize that trying to please everyone is an all consuming and never ending way of life. There is no way to please everyone. If the truth were revealed, our own best friends say things from time to time behind our backs about us that are negative.

There is a way to escape this cycle. Take the same energy it takes to react and respond negatively and rechannel it. By rechanneling this energy, happiness could be the result rather than guilt. All it requires to rechannel energy is to constantly work on staying pleasant regardless of the situation. Staying pleasant is a behavior easily achieved if you decide that it is time to get off the negative cycle of bad responses and reactions. Refocus the negative energy to become happier in your life.

The first thing to learn is to respond in any situation only with a smile. Not with words, with emotion, with body language -- but -- with only a smile. A good smile will neutralize any situation you face long enough for you not to respond negatively, (which has been part of your conditioning over time).

Smiling might seem fake at first. The smile you put on your face could feel forced. If it feels forced, it probably is! Don't force a smile; Let yourself relax in the face of a situation and let the emotional energy of the relaxation come out on your face.

Smiling is a lost art form. Smiling needs to be recaptured on the faces of people. All you need to do is look around you in the day to day hustle and bustle of living and you will see that people have lost the ability to smile. Rise to this challenge and you will see how much more pleasant your life will be if you simply start to smile.

The second thing to learn is to learn to breathe better -- instead of reacting quickly. Breathe -- count to ten...or to one hundred -- take a step back...do whatever you need to do to not react quickly to any situation. Take your time reacting and you will see how differently things will turn out.

If you are nervous, stressed, or tense, take two very long and very deep breaths. It should give you a quick, refreshing feeling of relaxing. If it doesn't, repeat the procedure until it does.

Simply applying these first two ideas will not only change your behavior, make you happier, and relieve your guilt, but they will help you to live longer. Quick reactions and responses do all kinds of negative things to your body chemistry, blood pressure, and blood sugar. Learning to stay pleasant instead of responding negatively or reacting quickly, will change your length of life to the better!

The third thing to learn is to not release your opinion, but show restraint. You will become happier in your life by staying pleasant through restraining yourself. This doesn't mean you have to "hold it all in," but most of the time you should "hold it in" until the urge to speak passes. You might find yourself in a better position with others. This position will feel quite differently than before. Instead of people avoiding conversations with you, they may seek you out because they know you are more restrained and happier.

YOU CAN BECOME
HAPPIER BY BEING
PLEASANT:

1. Instead of responding --
just smile.

2. Instead of reacting -- learn
to breathe better.

3. Instead of releasing your
opinion -- restrain yourself.

DAY 9: DOWNSIZE

Do you ever find yourself trying to find a place to store something you haven't been using, but don't have the courage to get rid of it? Life has a way of accumulating a bunch of stuff. All this "stuff" needs managed or it wears out too early, or breaks down at the wrong time. The more "stuff" we have, the more worry often goes along with it. It is no wonder that we have a hard time achieving happiness. We don't have the time to. All the "stuff" we accumulate zaps our time, energy, and emotion.

Because happiness is so often associated with "things," we accumulate more "stuff" to feel happy. The problem is we accumulate more thinking we are going to be happier -- but the happiness does not follow. We are then more likely to believe that happiness will never exist for us.

The best answer to the accumulation problem is to downsize your life. Instead of accumulating, get rid of a few things. Get your family involved. Talk it over with them. Help them see that, as a family, you have made life difficult and burdensome because of "needing this" or "just have to have" that. Striving to get more usually causes us to not be thankful for what we already have because what we already have never feels like it is enough. The only way to jump off this cycle is to make the immediate decision to downsize.

Downsizing means you make the decision to stop accumulating things where possible. There are always things you and your family need. There are also those things you really don't need, but it seems like life couldn't possibly go on without getting "it." It is in this category where accumulation needs to stop if you are going to ever achieve happiness in your life. There is always something more you could get. A new gadget, a toy, an appliance, or some technical advances are always temptations to accumulate more "things." Remember that the more things you have, the more time and money it requires to keep them running. Downsizing needs to be practical. Up grading your computer because of changing times is different from needing two or three computers. Trading cars for a better one is different from having to have three or four different cars because of the seasons and type of activity.

Downsizing means you learn to appreciate the things you already have. There is a way to downsize which requires very little thinking. If you know of something you want to buy, find something you already have similar to it. Now, clean it, mend it, or fix it. By doing this, you will get your hands on it and see that you really don't need to accumulate more "stuff," but simply enjoy the "stuff" you already have.

One of the reasons we accumulate so many different gadgets is because we think they will be better, easier, or improved over the last gadget we accumulated.

Downsizing does not necessarily mean you have to get rid of things -- it means to live with what you now have. If you live with what you have, the general courses of living will downsize your life naturally.

Downsizing means to take better care of the "stuff" you already have. Make it your desire to keep things tidy. By so doing you will learn that what you desire, you already have.

The old saying, "he changes cars whenever the oil needs changed" is often true with some people. They are so afraid of a break down out on the highway that they never enjoy or appreciate the vehicle they now have. Once you are caught up in fear, it will control your life. Nothing will ever be good enough or dependable enough. You will spend a fortune on "stuff" and never be happy.

The only answer is to take things as they come. If your car breaks down, take it in stride. Remember that when your car stops, so will you! Fix it when it is time. Learn to maintain things in a proper way, with a good balance. Take it one day at a time.

You can only drive one car at a time, live in one home at a time, and play with only one toy at a time. Downsizing your life could be something which blesses you more than you ever thought possible.

Become a downsizer rather than an accumulator.

DOWNSIZING MY LIFE IS AN IMPORTANT KEY TO HAPPINESS.

1. Make the decision to stop accumulating "stuff."

2. Appreciate the "stuff" you now have.

3. Take better care of the "stuff" you now have.

DAY 10: LOWER YOUR DEBT

Many of us are caught in a trap. As long as we keep running, we never feel trapped. Once we stop long enough, the panic of feeling caught by the trap we are in, catches up. Running on the tread mill of keeping ahead of feeling trapped is the game many play. It becomes the life many people live. The trap we are caught in is debt.

Whether you define debt as unsecured credit, bills past due, or even your mortgage loan, it is a concept, which controls many lives past what is necessary. Debt controls us, not because it is a phantom, but because it actually controls our decisions, our schedules, our spending, our lifestyles, and even our relationships. It is a downward spiral which catches many by surprise: You buy now thinking you have plenty of time to pay later, but later never really comes. The more you spend, the more you are extended. You pay the interest, (which is outrageous), and hope eventually to start paying on the principle. This becomes a trap because lifestyles become inflated, and you have to work another job or two to keep things paid. Because you have less time, your family ends up raising themselves, and your relationships suffer because you are out of the picture -- all due to too much debt.

This kind of life will never result in happiness -- but misery. Living with debt never brings any form of happiness. If you have to borrow to purchase something, you are putting yourself in danger of not achieving happiness in your life.

If you buy something on your credit card, which you can't pay off in full when the bill comes, you couldn't afford what you bought. We have learned to justify not paying it off by thinking we have several months to do so. This cycle goes on and on in homes around the world. People want desperately to be happy, but debt is robbing them of real, true happiness in their lives.

Lowering your debt is not some radical idea that will change your life drastically. It needs to be a decision to simply change the direction of how things are going in your life. Making the decision to lower your debt will begin the feeling of happiness which has eluded you all the while you have fallen into the debt trap.

Admitting that you have fallen into this trap and you are going to quit doing it, is the start.

Think in terms of lowering your debt as a decision. When you make the decision to lower your debt, you will not be prone to buy something on a credit card that you cannot pay off in 30 days. One way to immediately start lowering your debt is to quit getting yourself into debt. If you can't pay for it within the 30-day period you simply can't afford it.

Think in terms of lowering your debt as a project. Allow the whole concept of lowering your debt to replace the current urge you have to spend. It is the same emotional need, only now placed in a better position. If you are going to go about lowering your debt as a project, it is going to take the commitment of all parties involved. If your significant other has contributed to the debt, they are going to have to be part of the decision and the project.

Think in terms of lowering your debt as freedom, which will lead you to a happier life. The more you desire the freedom from debt, the greater you will be able to lower your debt and the happier you will be. Lowering your debt is not some all-consuming passion of wiping it out completely. It won't do you any good to see lowering your debt as a passion to wipe out all debt as soon as possible because you won't actually be changing how you live. People who are consumed with spending, who then are consumed with wiping out debt, usually go right back into debt again.

The idea of lowering your debt is to change your lifestyle and way of doing things over a long enough course of time that your habits, attitude, and lifestyle change.

This change will lead immediately to a happier life and multiply proportionately to the length of time lowering debt is pursued.

LOWERING YOUR DEBT WILL HELP LEAD TO A HAPPIER LIFE IF YOU THINK IN TERMS OF:

1. Lowering your debt as a decision.

2. Lowering your debt as a project.

3. **Lowering your debt as freedom.**

DAY 11: SIMPLIFY YOUR SYSTEMS

Life can get complicated. Schedules get so filled that families spend their lives running around to get the next thing on the list done. Running around costs money. Activities increase and so do personal spending and debt. The more you do, the more it costs; the more you have to work, the less time you have, the greater the guilt, and the more pronounced personal problems become. It goes without saying that happiness is gone.

Simplify. Instead of complicating life, start simplifying the systems you use in your life to manage what you do and where you go.

Simplifying is the only answer to life out of control. Simplifying will also provide you with almost immediate happiness. Simplifying your systems is a simple three-step approach.

Step #1: Live simpler by starting to limit your involvement. Give everyone in the family some choices. No one can be involved in everything that comes along, and no one should be involved in nothing but running the rest around. Simplifying does not mean you have a "designated driver" who doesn't deserve to have his or her own involvement. Don't let the kids play every sport. If you do, you run the risk of your children feeling like the whole family revolves around them. Just because Dad is the major breadwinner doesn't mean he shouldn't have to wait his turn at involvement either.

Simplifying your systems has to be fair to everyone in the family. Choose one or two sports, one or two hobbies, and one or two committees. Don't think in terms of everything for everyone. Have the family discuss their involvement together. Take the time to decide what is best for one -- and then -- discuss what is best for all. Use this opportunity to teach and explain the importance of simplifying life. Use it to help your family see how they need each other, more than an event, to be happy in their lives.

Step #2: Think simpler by being honest. Many of our complications come from our lack of courage to be honest with ourselves and with others. Fearing rejection of others and thereby saying "yes" when you should say "no" is not honest. Living by limits means that you have to be honest enough to set those limits in the first place. A lack of honesty causes us to deny the fact that our lives have become complicated beyond healthy limits. This lack of honesty is destructive because it never allows a person the freedom to say enough is enough.

When we fear how others might respond to our "saying no," we set ourselves up for failure. There is no way to please everyone, and unless we simplify our lives rather than allow things to become more complicated, we will always fail others -- and thereby bring to pass the very thing we are trying so hard to avoid.

Step #3: Act simpler by easing up. A complicated life is stressed, on the verge of burn out, and frustrated. It is a merry-go-round that people want desperately to get off. No one is ever able to get off, until they decide to. The best thing to do when faced with the complications of life is to ease up.

The natural tendency is to move faster, work harder, and get there first. The best thing is to do the opposite.

How many times have you rushed around only to be caught by a traffic accident ahead of you that slowed you down anyway? How about rushing to the airport, hurrying to the gate, pushing ahead to board first for a good seat, only to have the airplane unable to leave the gate because of heavy air traffic? The "hurry up to wait" scenario happens thousands of times per day. Your life will become simpler and happier if you choose to ease up.

Easing up is that kind of attitude which can affect your life deep down inside. It is one of the best things you can do for your relationships because almost every relationship needs a lot more ease in it, and a lot less intensity. Easing up is one of the best things you can do for your health. Both physically and mentally, easing up can do remarkable things for your wellness. Relaxing more and stressing less makes you healthier. Finally, easing up simply makes you happier. You will have the time and attitude to enjoy your life to the fullest -- that is the essence of happiness.

THERE ARE THREE STEPS TO SIMPLIFYING THE SYSTEMS OF YOUR LIFE:

Step #1:
Limit your involvement.

Step #2:
Be honest with yourself.

Step #3:
Ease up in all areas.

DAY 12: EAT LESS

Food actually brings people happiness. This kind of happiness is often a phantom because it is not lasting. Letting food become the point of your happiness is as dangerous -- actually more dangerous because it involves your physical health -- as allowing material things to become your source of happiness.

Food has a purpose. It is intended to provide your body with the energy to be productive. The productivity is the source of happiness, not the food that provides the energy. We are conditioned from the start of life with regard to food. Every happy moment seems to revolve around eating. Family time, holidays, Grandmother's house, dates, nights out, and business deals are times that result in much happiness and also involve food. It is no wonder many of us associate food with happiness.

It is also no wonder that so many negative times involve food as well. Family fights, holiday tension, and emotionally difficult memories happened around gathered times for eating.

Eating disorders are associated with control. Eating is often the only thing many people feel that they can control. Because of these reasons, one of the ways to achieve happiness in your life is to eat less.

Food is often considered an "emotional thing." Many things are associated with food. Both internally and externally, food is the source of much consideration. In this way we should be able to see that one of the ways to achieve happiness in life is by eating less. If this seems hard for you, consider applying some of these ideas:

1. Track what you eat. Make a list over the course of several weeks of all the things you eat each day. Don't forget a thing. Write down everything from the biggest to the smallest -- even that stick of chewing gum. After spending some weeks journaling, analyze your list. It will surprise you. Many of us eat much more than what we first imagine. Becoming more conscious of the things you eat will help you with the next step in this process.

Track how you feel when you eat. This should include how you feel before you eat, as you eat, and after you eat. Tracking requires you to be aware and honest about your eating.

The realization that will surface may be a revelation as to how you feel emotionally concerning food. If food is a substitute for happiness, your honesty will be the best help in revealing it, exposing it, and resolving it.

2. Get some information on food and nutrition that you can understand. We all need to eat better. Not everything available is understandable. The important thing is for you to understand the information and your own body.

It is important is to apply good information a little at a time. Trying to go too far too fast usually ends up in frustration. Doing a little at a time and applying new information in steps is the best way to change your life. Learn and apply at your own pace. It is the only way to change your way of thinking -- and your way of life.

3. Cut all your portions in half. After becoming

more conscious of what you eat, now look things over and think it through. Think in terms of what you would normally eat, and cut that amount in half. This needs to be a long-term commitment. It will immediately make you feel better about yourself. This feeling will result in some much-needed happiness.

The decision to cut your portions in half will help your consciousness be put to a practical test. Feeling a little hungry more often is a good thing. Too many people try to "fill up." We don't need to fatten ourselves, only feed ourselves.

4. Lose some weight over the course of time. <u>Don't panic -- if you do the first three steps -- this will happen naturally!</u> People who lose weight feel better about themselves, and even feel better physically. You will also notice a new-found happiness. This will happen to you. Do it over the course of time. However, if you apply this principle of happiness -- don't rush it! Let this be a life long project.

IF YOU EAT LESS YOUR WHOLE LIFE WILL BE HAPPIER.
1. Track what you eat.

2. Get some information you can use and understand.

3. Cut all your portions in half.

4. Don't rush weight loss.

DAY 13: LOOK FOR THE BEST

It has never really been established that people are negative by nature. It is natural to want to feel better about yourself, and negativity is often the result. Negativity is an attempt people use to feel better about themselves. The problem is, the result is not lasting. It never results in happiness.

The reason people criticize or talk about others negatively behind their backs is because of their own feelings of insecurity. People criticize others to feel better about themselves. The more people criticize, the smaller they really become, thus increasing their insecurity.

The best way to happiness is to train yourself to go the other way. Instead of going down the negative road, go down the positive one. This journey is as simple as looking for the best, rather than the worst, in every situation and person.

Looking for the best in people and situations requires you to make the resolve that you are going to begin. There is bad in the best of any situation or any person, and there is good in the worst of any situation or any person. What you look for is what you are going to find. This puts the effort on each of us to change our lives in this way. If you resolve to look for the best, the change in your life will happen immediately. If you are looking for the best in people and situations, others will be attracted to you. They will immediately see that you are a very special person. The resolve you make to look for the best will become contagious to others around you. Happiness will be at your disposal because you will realize that there is much positive in the life you thought was always negative.

Taking the high road when thinking about and talking of others will bring certain happiness because you are no longer pulled down, or pulled into the insecure feelings of others.

Looking for the best in people and situations requires you to take time to cultivate both people and situations. Although positive things aren't always at the surface, it is always just below the surface of any person or situation. All that it takes for the positive to be brought out is for it to be emphasized. Because life is so rushed, cultivation is not allowed to take place. There are many positives in the life of each person; we just don't take the time to bring it out. There are also positive things about situations, but life moves so fast that we need answers first and cultivation second. Once you decide to cultivate life, you will see the positive side to everything.

The idea that we reap what we sow is more than just an agricultural scenario. It illustrates the fact that we receive back what we put into something. Rather than using people and cultivating things, we need to use things and cultivate people. Every single person you meet has unbelievable possibilities.

Looking for the best in people and situations requires you to speak positive words to others. Sometimes you have to confess with your mouth what you are looking for. Looking for the best in people and situations requires us to speak positively with our mouths. It is important to affirm people. Let it flow. People are hungry to be affirmed in their lives. If you look for the best in others, you need to confess it to them when you find it. Don't use the opportunity to criticize, affirm them with no other motive.

Looking for the best in people and situations requires you to speak positive words about others behind their backs. Don't just speak positive words to their faces, say the same things behind their back. Breaking out of the pattern of negativity will bring immediate happiness, but when you begin to confess positive words to others, you will spread the happiness around into the lives of others.

If people hear you say positive things about others behind their backs, they will soon assume you do the same for them. The trust you will build will bring you much happiness throughout your future.

LOOKING FOR THE BEST IN OTHERS REQUIRES YOU TO:

1. Look for the best, rather than the worst in every situation.

2. Take the time to cultivate.

3. Speak positive words to others.

4. Speak positive words about others.

DAY 14: GET RID OF GUILT

Guilt is a thief. It robs you of health, wealth, and happiness. There are people more prone to guilt than others, but everyone carries too much guilt. Guilt is a waste of time. People who carry guilt either don't admit to responsibility, or admit to too much responsibility. There is very little middle ground with people caught up in guilt. That is why we need to get rid of it.

Get rid of guilt by clearing your conscious. Is there something that needs to be resolved somewhere in your life? If there is, then resolve it. Do whatever is necessary to resolve the issue, which has caused the guilt you have been carrying. It may require a phone call, a trip, a letter, or standing over a grave marker. Remember that resolving guilt is a two way street. If your resolve involves a person, remember that if they are living, they may not want a resolve. That is why clearing your conscious is the most important thing. You can only clear your own conscious; you can't clear someone else's.

Once you have tried to resolve it...then let it go. Even if you were not able to resolve it to any level of satisfaction -- at least you tried. Trying is the whole key to a clear conscious. Let it go. Whether guilt goes either way (you are defensive or you are blaming yourself), it is important to let it go. The only one guilt hurts is you. You can play mind games with others, but you really are not hurting them the way you might think. The only one you hurt is you.

Remind yourself that guilt is a mind game -- one that you are playing with and on yourself. Mind games are usually something we blame others for. When guilt is involved, you are playing it with yourself. Anyone else involved in your equation is a victim of your own making. Even if someone has hurt you, your use of guilt on him or her is making them your victim.

Accept things the way they are and move on with life. Acceptance may be the hardest part of getting rid of guilt. Acceptance is also the way which happiness comes. Unless you accept things as they are, you will never be at peace with yourself or your life. Even then, you have to move on with life. Much of life is learning to deal with uncomfortable circumstances.

YOU HAVE TO LET GO OF
GUILT TO BE HAPPY.
TO DO THIS:

1. Resolve your problems
with others while possible.

2. Let go of those things
which can't be resolved.

3. Remind yourself that guilt
is a mind game, which you
play with yourself.

4. Accept things the way they
are and move on with life.

DAY 15: CHERISH OTHERS

Of the things we take for granted, the top of the list would have to be EACH OTHER. Rarely do we invest the type of emotional energy necessary to yield dividends in any relationship we have. It takes work <u>not</u> to take each other for granted because so many of the things we do in our lives requires certain amounts of self service. As long as we are caught in these patterns, we will never have the depth of relationships possible between people. The difference between taking people for granted and not taking people for granted is the capacity we have to cherish others.

Fear of hurt keeps us from truly enjoying each other the way we should. Everyone has been hurt at some level by others. The previous hurt can often get in the way of enjoying others because of a fear of the hurt.

Cherishing others requires a certain amount of risk. The amount of effort and openness directly results in the amount of happiness received.

Happiness is missing when we take others for granted because affection, admiration, affirmation, or love can not be shared from person to person. People need a positive environment for the giving and receiving of love to be truly happy in their lives. When people are taken for granted, these avenues of love don't exist. When love is absent, happiness will be also.

<u>Cherishing others is simple, but requires the application of three simple rules:</u>

First, treat others the way you want to be treated.

So many times we don't take the time to apply this simple principle of success. This is not an idea that can be applied to your life on a sporadic basis. It has to be a consistently executed habit of your life. You have to resolve that whether you are driving, exercising, shopping or working that you are going to treat everyone you come into contact with as you want him or her to treat you. This will mean that you cut people slack, give them space, and even make excuses for their failings.

The up side to the execution of this principle is it will change your life! Happiness will be the result of cherishing others in this way.

Second, treat those older than you the way you want others to treat your parents. It is easy to mistreat people older by focussing in upon their weaknesses. How different we feel if the person mistreated were parents. That is the transference we need. Think in terms of the respect and care we want others to give our own parents and then transfer those feelings into your own situation.

Your ability to apply this point will help you see people in a much different light. Being able to personalize and internalize relationships in a positive sense will help your ability to relate to everyone on a day to day basis.

Third, treat those younger the way you would want others to treat your children. Those youngsters you come into contact with who get on your nerves are someone's children. How differently most of us treat other people's kids! The reason is, we are not bonded to them the way their parents are -- nor do we understand them the way their parents do. The way to learn to cherish them -- even those who really get on your nerves -- is to realize they are someone's children.

How do you want people like you to think of and treat your kids? Transfer the feeling in a positive way. Because we know our children so well, we see them differently than other people do. The same is true of other's children as well. Everyone deserves our utmost respect for how they are treated. Making the decision to do better in this regard will help your own loved ones. They will reap from others what you have sowed in your relationships.

These three simple rules are sure to change your attitude toward others and help open up happiness in your life regardless of the people in it. Working these rules is as easy as just starting. Do it today!

---

3 RULES OF CHERISHING OTHERS:

<u>Rule #1</u>: Treat others the way you want to be treated.

<u>Rule #2</u>: Treat those older the way you would want others to treat your parents.

<u>Rule #3</u>: Treat those younger the way you would want others to treat your children.

DAY 16: SAVE SOME MONEY

It doesn't matter how much money you make -- much or little, or in between -- you will always figure out a way to spend it. When people move through the stages of life they often think in terms of making more and preparing for the future, but it always seems like there is something to absorb the extra that "might have been."

Frustration can develop if you have tried faithfully to save some money, only to have it used up in an emergency or a spur of the moment purchase. This frustration is often just below the surface of every conversation you have concerning money.

Frustrations abound even more when you consider our culture. Every time you turn around there is another option for spending money. Grocery stores package themselves to do more than just feed you; they are intent on separating you from your money. The same is true of car dealerships, shopping malls, and super stores. It is almost impossible to save any money today. It is better to admit it up front and then try some new approaches, than it is to think there is something wrong with you.

The most important thing to remember about saving money is: IT IS NOT HOW MUCH, BUT HOW OFTEN. The key word is consistency. Simply put -- "do the math." The amount has always been the thing that gets us hung up. We think that a little bit on a consistent basis does not add up to much. Nothing could be further from the truth. The key idea of saving is not how much, but how often. Look past the old things which used to get you hung up on not saving and determine that you are going to save a little bit on a regular basis. Set it up, then stick with it!

Another thing to remember is DON'T EVER TOUCH YOUR SAVINGS EXCEPT FOR INVESTMENT PURPOSES. Let it grow... Let it grow.... Let it grow! The problem most people face with regard to savings is their inability to leave their hands off it. Let it be the first amount you put aside each time you receive income. It won't seem like you have much for a long time. Leave it alone anyway. After you start to see it accumulating, leave it alone. Let it grow. No matter what kind of need you have, leave your savings alone. See it as something that is completely off limits to you.

Not leaving it alone is the mistake most people make when it comes to savings. They see money accumulate but eventually find a way to justify spending it. In our consumer-oriented culture, there will always be a way to spend money. We justify spending it.

When it comes to happiness, you will eventually see how much comfort saving will be for you. It is important to ENJOY THE BENEFITS OF SAVINGS BY REALIZING YOU HAVE A SAFETY NET. Although you have a commitment to yourself not to touch your savings, it should be used as an emotional safety net to help free up your anxiety about the future. As your savings grows it then will be become your security of the future. Remember money can never be a permanent sense of security. This concept is merely transitional in developing security in your life.

<u>Money, as such, should not be your emotional support</u>. Money is actually a symbol of something greater. Money is the symbol of your ability to be work, earn and save. Money saved means you are productive and

successful. Let it work for you in this way.

People with a feeling of a safety net, and a sense of security about the future, are people who are able to be happier in their lives. This is not to say that happiness is based upon money -- actually, nothing could be further from the truth. The ability to save money in this way has more to do with building your sense of purpose, destiny, and discipline than it has to do with money. Saving some money has to do with determination, commitment and discipline. Happiness will develop as determination, commitment and discipline are developed.

It is never too late to start saving some money. Don't put it off any longer. Just because you didn't start years ago when you could have accumulated a fortune does not mean you should not start now. Saving is more than just accumulating money; it will give you a whole new level of vitality for your life.

LEARNING TO SAVE MONEY WILL BRING HAPPINESS NOT BECAUSE OF THE MONEY YOU WILL HAVE SAVED, BUT BECAUSE OF THE DETERMINATION AND DISCIPLINE YOU WILL HAVE APPLIED TO YOUR LIFE.

DAY 17: DRINK WATER

Water has some amazing qualities to it. Since most of our physical bodies are comprised of water, it is important for us to drink plenty of it. The medical standpoint alone has sufficient research to show us that we don't drink enough water.

Water is a cleanser. It was put on earth for a purpose. All of us have a natural tendency to become thirsty. Water is the most natural and beneficial thing to quench our natural thirst.

When dealing with happiness, water has some amazingly symbolic qualities to it. Drinking water will not only make you healthier, it will make you happier.

The more water you drink, the less likely you will drink chemical laden beverages. The things we consume can't be doing us any good physically. The same is true mentally. Sugar, caffeine, chemicals, dyes, alcohol, and others all have their ways of affecting our physical/mental systems. A great way to overcome their effect on us is to bypass their use by drinking more water. You will begin to notice some initial withdrawal depending on the type of beverage you use. During these times of headaches, shakes, and even more profound withdrawal symptoms, remind yourself that the pain is temporary. You are on the road to a better life. You are beginning a new life. Getting these chemicals out of your system will help you physically -- realizing they are out of your system will help you feel better about yourself and happier with your life.

The more water you drink, the more cleansed you

will feel. Because our bodies are comprised of so much water, it is important to keep all the systems working to their optimum capacity. Sadly, very few people put this idea to work. We usually allow the hustle and bustle of our lives to dictate whatever is available to drink. The drink of choice becomes whatever will help us to get through the day. Through this scenario our lives become a day to day struggle just to get through however we can. We don't have to live this way! We can have fulfillment, love, and happiness beyond our dreams, but it all starts with a few small steps. In this case, it is to drink more water. It will cleanse your body -- and -- if you allow the idea that you are drinking more water and less of everything else -- it will cleanse your soul as well.

The more water you drink, the better you will feel about yourself. Water is the most overlooked area of good health. It is completely natural and an important part of good health. You could even say water is a "God thing." How else could something tasteless, colorless, and (supposed to be) odorless be so important for you.

Fill your sip cup with water rather than your beverage of choice and you will notice positive changes occur in your life. These positive changes will affect you physically and mentally.

It will require a conscious effort on your part to drink more water. It won't naturally happen. You will have to make the decision and then stick with it. Start by setting goals as to how much water you are going to drink during certain times of the day.

Drink water regularly and with a thankful heart. This will insure that you are on the right track for happiness. Teach yourself to enjoy water. Make a commitment to not drink current beverages in lieu of water.

What does water have to do with happiness? The answer is illustrative as well as practical. Practically, we need to drink more water on a daily basis to fight off diseases before they begin. Illustratively, making a decision to drink more water on a daily basis helps us to realize that the important things in our lives we often take for granted -- things like -- water and (happiness).

DRINKING WATER WILL BRING HAPPINESS IN BOTH PHYSICAL AND SYMBOLIC WAYS.

1. When you drink more water you will likely absorb less chemicals which come from other beverages.

2. Water cleanses your body and your soul.

3. Water is natural and will help you feel better about yourself.

DAY 18: NOTICE LITTLE THINGS

The rush of life causes us to let the best part of life go unnoticed. The pace we live usually results in our constant frustration of never getting the things done we wanted to, and the exhausted, burned out feeling that accompanies it. Not only are we not happy, but (sad to say) we are miserable on the inside. This inner misery is not something we can adequately put our finger on, so it creates a cycle of "cause and effect" which we fail to overcome. It is a miserable ride on a merry-go-round that is going too fast to just jump off -- and keeps us just dizzy enough to not know which direction is safe to lean.

The way to get off the merry-go-round of a hectic pace of life and retrieve your happiness is to begin noticing the little things you are now ignoring.

Noticing the little things in your life will help you to slow down. Slowing down might be the last thing in the world you think you can do. It is the only thing you should do. Regardless of family, work, and other demands, the only way to regain your balance, and hence your happiness, is to slow down. Noticing the little things will help you to do so. Take the time to enjoy the little things: Eat slower and enjoy each bite -- taste the flavor; Drink slower and enjoy the feeling of it going down your throat; Drive slower and enjoy the landscape; Walk slower and watch a dog's expression around an owner who loves him; Think slower and enjoy coming up with a new idea; Live slower and watch a child on a playground.

Noticing a child on a playground will change your life. It is one of those little things that get overlooked. A child running from playground equipment to playground equipment does something rarely seen in life -- he runs from the soul. Watch a child at play and you will see that simple abandon we have all lost. Recover that spirit. It is easily recovered if we determine to start noticing the little things in life we have been over looking.

Noticing the little things in life will help you feel more thankful. The more thankful you can be for what you have, the more content you will become in every area of your life. Thankfulness always leads to happiness.
It also helps you to not take people and situations so much for granted. When we take things for granted, we don't treat them with the reverence they deserve. It comes back on us as well because we usually get back what we invest in both relationships and situations. When we take people and situations for granted, we are usually taken for granted ourselves.

Noticing the little things in life will force you to notice and express appreciation for those around you. Noticing the little things you appreciate in those around you will be a great benefit to you. Most of the time we are caught up in self-service. Noticing the little things that you appreciate will change the direction of how you think regarding others. Don't be surprised if people don't take you seriously at first because it is rare for anyone to think of others first. Thinking of others first is such a rarity that people won't know how to take it. Putting others first on a consistent basis will do unbelievable good to all of your relationships. It will also help you to get your eyes off of yourself. Selflessness leads to happiness. Selfishness leads to loneliness and isolation.

You can create your own sense of happiness just by

noticing the little things. Start right now. Start noticing the little things in your life. As you notice them, begin to appreciate them. Express your thankfulness in your own attitude. Let that new attitude rise up in and spring out of your life. Happiness is the new feeling you will experience just by starting to notice the little things.

The reason the little things go unnoticed is because we choose to ignore them. We often think of the little things in life as insignificant. This thought process is what causes us to go through life as unhappy. We are always looking ahead to the next big thing, all the while ignoring the little things which could become big things if they were only allowed to develop in our lives. A lot of potential happiness gets wasted this way.

NOTICE THE LITTLE THINGS IN LIFE:

1. It will help you slow down.

2. It will make you more thankful.

3. It will enrich your relationship to others and make you much happier in your life.

DAY 19: WASTE SOME TIME

Studies indicate that people today have more money than time. If these studies are current, wasting some time is the last thing anyone would be willing to do. Yet wasting time could be the greatest thing to do to regain some happiness.

Wasting some time has more to do with the mental feeling of freeing yourself up, than it does destroying your life by throwing out your schedule. Many people need to make some serious life changes if they are ever going to achieve any degree of happiness.

We are all too busy. We hurry here and there. We are trying to please too many people. The result is frustration, burn out, and stress. Seriously considering a career or job change may be the only way many people will ever achieve happiness.

If you have to change jobs just to waste a little time, then you should do it! Money is never more important than your time -- and time is the only thing that will contribute to your happiness. If your life leaves you constantly worn out and torn down, you need to start wasting a little time.

You need to get a little bored once in a while. Until you do, you won't have that feeling of looking forward to work. Unless you look forward to your work, you won't ever be as productive as you need to be at work. You won't ever really be happy either.

Wasting some time renews your desire to work. The suggestion is not to waste all your time, just a little time once in a while. Plan for time to waste -- when you will have nothing at all to do.

There is a great fear to wasting time. Even though you work hard at work, it is often the transference that causes us to make every minute count. If you work for someone who expects you to be "on the job" 24 hours a day, then you need to find another job. Your job should never "own you." A job is a job. You work to keep food on the table. If you have fallen into the great lie -- (your company couldn't survive without you) -- you need the ultimate vocational test: Waste a little personal time and see if it affects your ability to do your job.

Wasting some time refreshes your sense of perspective. When you fill up every minute with things to do, you can easily lose your perspective of even why you are doing all the things you are doing. Planning some time where you don't have anything planned will give some time to think, heal, renew and refresh.

Happiness is lost when you lose your sense of perspective. Regaining your perspective will give you a great shot at gaining happiness. The way to regain is to do nothing...nothing at all.

Wasting some time will revive your balance. Inner balance is what creates the possibility of happiness. A person out of balance is never happy until balance is achieved again. The need to waste some time comes from the inner knowledge that balance has been lost. During the time you are wasting some time your balance is being revived.

Not having anything to do will not seem natural.

This unnatural feeling is good. It causes you to stay sharp and in touch with your feelings. This kind of emotional/mental state is good when you are trying to revive something lost in your life.

If you have any kind of health problem, wasting some time is the thing that will help restore you the most -- especially if you waste some time with someone you love.

Spending time with those you love is not a waste of time at all -- but -- it would be interesting how people who work too much, who aren't really happy, and who have lost their center, are also people who deep down see time spent with family as a waste of time because it is not productive. These are people who constantly open up their briefcase, check the e-mail, or return phone calls, and call it all "family time." People like this need to waste some time and realize they are doing it!

WASTING SOME TIME WILL BRING HAPPINESS IN YOUR LIFE BECAUSE:

1. It renews your desire to work. Plan some time to do nothing.

2. It refreshes your sense of perspective. Plan some time to get bored.

3. It revives your balance. Waste some time with someone you love.

DAY 20: CHILL OUT

Stress and pressure can cause us to be in a constant state of tension. Tension prevents us from ever being relaxed enough to be happy. Regardless of the reason for your tension, it can be relieved in your life. All you have to do is make a definite decision to chill out.

Whenever you catch yourself getting stressed out -- stop in your tracks. Don't let yourself live under stress. Stop and analyze your life. Make changes, adjust attitudes, redo and renew yourself -- but don't go on living stressed out. Don't stress out. Chill out instead.

The kind of stress that causes tension that affects your attitude will indirectly affect your relationships as well. When you are under pressure, you are likely to treat those around you who love you with contemptible behavior. The only way to deal with your unacceptable behavior toward those you love is to stop in your tracks and change your attitude. Apologize, ask forgiveness, and change your behavior. Unless you do these things, your life can unravel quickly. We all need a group of loving people around us at all times. Don't alienate your group of support by treating them badly because you are under stress. Chill out instead.

Don't take yourself too seriously. The greatest way to chill yourself out is to stay aware of those times you take yourself too seriously. Most of us do take ourselves too seriously. Subsequently, we take our jobs too seriously, our careers too seriously, our family pride too seriously, and every area of our lives too seriously.

Tune in to your behavior. Know when you are

taking things too seriously. You will do yourself a great service by realizing when you are taking things emotionally too far. You will also be helping those you love to live happier lives.

The way to avoid the tension that comes from taking yourself too seriously is to laugh at yourself. Laugh often and laugh loudly at yourself. Don't be afraid to be self-deprecating. The less seriously you take yourself, the less stress you induce on your own life. Take a step back often to look at yourself. If you take a step back, often you will see how seriously you have been taking everything. The look you see will amuse you.

Chilling out means that you have to cool yourself off. Tension has the tendency to cause you to become all heated up, and chilling out means to cool yourself off. You cool yourself off by practicing some restraint with your reactions to things. The more worked up you get, the more worked up you will be. The more cooled off you get, the more relaxed you will be. If the goal is happiness, chilling out by cooling off is the only direction you should go. Letting yourself "go off" like many people do, causes tensions to rise, and you end up getting stressed out over many things. The tighter you wind yourself up, the more stress you will experience in your work, your home, and in all your relationships.

You can chill out if you choose to. It is completely your own decision. Make yourself aware of how you are coming across to people. Do you seem like a person stressed out and ready to pounce? Be honest with yourself.

If you chill out and change your attitude people will be attracted to you. So many people juggle stress that they are repelled by people who can't handle stress. The opposite is true of people who are able to chill out and let go of their tension. These people are able to lead happy and relaxed lives.

Chilling out is an immediate, purposeful way to handle your stress. Stress and pressure have a profound effect on your physical and mental health. It takes constant attention to recognize a propensity to be stressed out over situations. It also takes honesty. It is more important to chill out and stay steady than to be prideful and defensive. Defensiveness and denial leads to stress and pressure producing a profound negative impact on your life and those around you. Chill out quickly and be relieved from the pressure and the guilt that comes from hurting those around you.

HAPPY PEOPLE KNOW THAT THEY NEED TO RECOGNIZE WHEN THEY ARE CARRYING STRESS AND "CHILL OUT."

1. When you feel you are stressed out, just stop in your tracks.

2. Don't take yourself too seriously.

3. Laugh at yourself. Laugh often.

4. Cool off.

DAY 21: FACE YOUR FEAR

Most of the things we worry about never even come close to coming to pass. That means we waste a lot of time thinking about needless things. The root of our worry is always in our fears. Fear has a way of robbing us of a quality of life -- life that is ours to enjoy -- a lifestyle, which should bring us happiness. Instead, life brings us worry and fear. The more we fear, the greater our fear becomes. Emotionally speaking, fear is a growing entity, which consumes our energy. The greater our fear, the greater it will be. That is why we have to face our fear. By facing it, we instantly overcome it!

Face fear by being honest that fear exists for you. This might be the hardest part about-facing your fear. Honesty is the only thing that will help you face fear. If you go through life denying the existence of fear, or not being completely honest about its existence, you will never be able to face it. Further, if you go through life not being honest about your fear, you will put those around you in danger because they are assuming fear doesn't exist.

Fear can cause us to be cautious, which is not bad in its own right, but it can often cause us to be unpredictable, which can bring harm to those you love if they aren't expecting it.

Fear is hard to track down by others if they want to confront you about it. The only way to face fear is not through them -- it has to be through you, and that is only by being honest about the things you fear.

The healthy kinds of fear which motivate us to look

before crossing the road are very different from the kinds of fear people carry through their lives; those fears secretly steal a person's potential for happiness because of their constantly gnawing fear of things.

We face fear by not avoiding it. The natural response to fear is to avoid anything similar to the thing feared. The opposite is to try to face the fear, overcome it, and allow happiness back into your life. Don't avoid the thing you fear.

The natural tendency, which causes you to avoid the thing you fear, is not a natural defensive mechanism at all -- it is a mechanism of your own making. You have created the avoidance yourself. Avoiding the thing you fear only prolongs the inevitable confrontation with your fear. Confrontation will come sometime in your life.

We face fear by getting professional help, if necessary, to overcome it. Professional help is often avoided because it makes us feel weak. If honesty prevails, you will admit that fear makes you weak to begin with. The help you receive from a competent professional could be the way back to the road of happiness. It is a small price to pay (which is the price of your pride) to face your fear and get back to happiness.

Some people don't get professional help because they think they can handle it themselves. Getting the help of a professional is not the last resort of a desperate and weak person; it is a smart move by a person who is tired of their fear robbing them of happiness.

We face fear by relaxing our attitudes rather than tensing up. If you could teach yourself to relax a little more, the problem of fear would not be as intense. Our inner lives are becoming more fearful or more relaxed. There is no middle ground because life is constantly changing.

If you don't relax, fear will be a constant companion because the fear won't let you relax. You will always be on guard protecting yourself from your own hidden fears.

Relax and enjoy the experience of being a little more vulnerable, a lot more happier, and set free from your fear.

FACING YOUR FEARS WILL HELP YOU BECOME MORE RELAXED AND HAPPIER.

1. We face our fear by being honest with ourselves.

2. We face our fears by not avoiding our fears.

3. We face our fears by working with a professional if necessary.

4. We face our fear by relaxing.

DAY 22: CLIP YOUR CREDIT CARDS

The way things are done in a society often becomes "culture." Culture is created because the participants have an acceptable way of doing things, which has become a part of their lives. Each culture has its own unique qualities, which defines them.

The way of doing things in a culture can seem quite weird to people coming in from outside of the culture. The people within a culture seem perfectly at ease doing things the way they do because culture is a part of a person's way of life. People don't know any different until, over time, the way they do things in their society is changed and shifted. A different culture is introduced, but only to the extent that a person's ability to adapt to a new way of doing things is not impaired.

Part of our day-to-day culture involves the use of credit cards. Credit cards can be a tremendous convenience since so many things can be expedited by using a credit card.

This kind of advantage is not in and of itself wrong. It does not rob you of quality or happiness of life.

Where things go wrong is when you don't pay the credit card bill off when it comes every month. When you allow a payment to slide for whatever reason, you are robbing yourself. If you can't afford to pay it off financially, then you are spending too much money on things that should wait.

Happiness will never be yours if you are living on

your credit card. Our culture has made credit card living a way of life. If you want happiness in your life, you are going to have to go against the current of society's norms in this area.

Buying on credit is a bad habit. As acceptable as it is, getting something you can't pay off in 30 days when the credit card bill comes is bad business. The more you carry a balance the more it seems normal, but the whole scenario of buying on credit is bad news. Clip your credit cards and throw them away. It will sting at first because you won't be getting everything you want, but very soon you will begin enjoying the thing you need the greatest -- inner happiness.

Buying on credit when you don't have the money to pay for it is irresponsible. Just because everyone practices irresponsibility doesn't make it right. If you continue to buy on credit, you won't be able to know what your financial picture is. When this happens, it is easier to buy more and more, thinking it somehow will take care of itself. It won't -- Not until you clip your credit cards and throw them away.

Buying on credit makes you think in terms of what you don't have rather than what you do have. When you are always driven by what you don't have, you will never take the opportunity to be thankful for what you do have. This attitude is destructive to you and those around you. If you always have to buy something to be happy, you will never be satisfied with anything. The more you buy, the less likely you will ever be happy. Soon you will feel trapped, depressed, and unfulfilled. Clip your credit cards and throw them away. Then buy only those things you can pay for with cash.

Buying on credit sets yourself up for failure. Buying

now thinking you will pay later sure makes some assumptions about tomorrow which is not ours to assume. Buying on credit holds our "tomorrows" hostage. Not really knowing where the money is going to come from should be warning enough not to buy. The stress and pressure from the credit card bill alone should keep us from setting ourselves up like that from month to month.

Learning to pay cash for things will cause you many inconveniences you are not used to, but you will quickly notice how much easier it is to track things. You will instantly be able to see where you are spending your money. It will quickly reveal your strengths and weaknesses in regard to many areas of your life. Credit cards cause you to live is a phantom world. Credit is not the real thing. Restore your happiness -- clip your credit cards.

CLIP UP YOUR CREDIT CARDS AND THROW THEM AWAY -- CREDIT ROBS YOU OF HAPPINESS.

1. Buying on credit is a bad habit.

2. Buying on credit is irresponsible.

3. Buying on credit takes away a thankful attitude.

4. Buying on credit sets yourself up for failure.

DAY 23: MANAGE YOUR ANGER

Angry people are rarely ever happy. Not because they can't be happy, but because the same mind set which causes a person to deny and cover up their anger, is the same attitude which prevents happiness. Anger robs you of happiness because it consumes the same exact emotional energy, which would allow you to be happy.

Everyone experiences some level of anger. Because anger is often associated with violence, we all shy away from admitting to being angry. We are also concerned about how admitting to anger would affect our image in the eyes of others.

The reason we need to quit denying anger is so that we can start managing it instead. As long as you deny you are angry, you won't be able to manage the anger, which exists. We all must admit to anger and admit to when there are times we are angry.

Managing your anger also requires taking responsibility for what your anger does. This would include the damage of the past and the chaos of today. Taking responsibility means that you realize that anger, which is not managed, is not acceptable behavior. Further, that you and you alone accept the responsibility for the damage of the past. You will no longer blame someone or something else. There may be a price to be paid for accepting the responsibility, but it is important that you do -- because -- until you do, you will not be able to move on with your life.

Accepting the responsibility for your anger might mean you have to actually pay restitution for the result of your anger. Don't run from, deny, or get out of this. Sometimes the only way to really learn from a situation is when the results of your behavior have to cost you something.

Don't let other people get out of accepting their responsibility either. There are times when people shouldn't be let off the hook, and they know it. In these cases, don't let them off the hook just because you would like to do them a favor.

Next, you need to learn to take a step back, instead of a step toward situations, which make you angry. Counting to ten (or a hundred) does not always work. When you are faced with angry situations, you must choose to take a step back and catch your breath. This will give you some space and time to get your thinking back on track. By doing so, you will have accomplished 90% of what managing anger is all about.

After you have taken a step back and given the situation which irritates you some time and space -- it is important to apply a key principle of anger management which is often the hardest: Make excuses for others. When you begin to quit making excuses for yourself, you will then be able to make excuses for others. A true sense of empathy is the goal of this concept. When you are able to empathize with others, you will be able to manage your anger at will.

The behavior model, which is called the golden rule, goes like this: "Do unto others the way you would have them do unto you." Working on this one simple rule will be all you really need to manage your anger.

Giving and receiving affirmation is important to

maintain a positive sense of self-esteem. Anger has a way of causing suspicion and distrust between people because of how intense it can be and how long it can be carried. Managing anger can bring a sense of relief to people because they can deal with it and move on with life.

Being more open about dealing with and managing anger could allow your relationships to be in a constant state of renewal. People will consider you more approachable because you are dealing with your own issues in a more positive -- and vulnerable -- way. It will be a positive experience both to you and those around you, which always helps on the road to happiness.

HAPPINESS IS NEVER PRESENT WHEN ANGER IS -- MANAGE YOUR ANGER AND GET BACK ON THE ROAD TO HAPPINESS.

1. Stop denying anger.

2. Take responsibility for your anger.

3. Take a step back.

4. Make excuses for others.

5. "Do unto others the way you would have them do unto you."

DAY 24: ADMIT TO WEAKNESSES

We all know we have strengths and weaknesses. The juggling act of "image" stands in the way of honesty regarding strengths and weaknesses. It also stands in the way of happiness. We can't keep the secret forever; it is foolish to try. Identifying and admitting to weaknesses is a positive way to gain more happiness.

Admitting your weaknesses keeps your feet firmly on the ground. Regardless of success and failure, admitting to weaknesses helps us keep ourselves grounded. We need to keep ourselves stable regardless of the things life has for us. We can keep things constant if we are reminded there are constantly things on which we need to be working.

Admitting your weaknesses gives you a place to relate to others. Everyone has strengths and weaknesses. If you go through life emphasizing to yourself your strengths, but not your weaknesses, you will never be able to relate to others in important ways. You will never be able to empathize and feel for others. The ability to relate to others is directly related to your capacity to be happy. The inability to relate to others has the same effect. Admitting your weaknesses gives you the opening to start relating to others.

Admitting your weaknesses opens up a commonality between people. This occurs because the person that benefits the greatest from admitting weaknesses is you. The humility of admitting weaknesses gives you an attitude, which is much more open than you could ever know. People will be able to relate to you. You will no longer be alienated from others. You will also find others who have similar weaknesses to yours. The commonality of weaknesses often brings a corporation of strength.

Admitting your weaknesses gives you something personal to continue to work on. Working on your own life should be a happy experience. Working on your weaknesses should be a satisfying and fulfilling process. That thing we fight the most can become our greatest ally. Weaknesses are not as difficult to work on as always thought. Admitting, facing, and working on weaknesses can bring positive reinforcement to life.

ADMITTING YOUR WEAKNESSES IS 95% OF THE WORK! ADMITTING YOUR WEAKNESSES:

1. Keeps your feet on the ground.

2. Gives you a place to relate to others.

3. Allows a commonality between people.

4. Gives you something to work on.

DAY 25: THINK ONLY POSITIVE

Negative thinking leads to negative living. Positive thinking leads to positive living and a happy life. The process of thinking positive requires a forceful commitment.

Happiness is a decision. The lack thereof is based upon the decision that one desires a less happy, more negative life. What it comes down to is simple -- happiness is a personal choice based upon inner desire, not contingent on someone or something else. You can be happy in the most miserable circumstances, or miserable in the most exceptional circumstances. Which way it will be is completely up to you.

Happiness is not based upon a job or career, spouse or relationship, money or fortune. It is a choice. The choice is whether or not you chose to develop a positive outlook on life.

Developing a positive outlook and happiness in life means you have to commit yourself to looking for the best, not the worst, in everyone and everything. There is bad in the best of any person and there is good in the worst; what you look for in someone is what you are going to find. The same thing is true in situations. The easiest way to get by is being negative because it is hard work to look for the best. But, looking for the best is worth it for the happy life which results.

The reality is -- what you look for is what you find! What is it you are finding in others? We usually pick apart in others what our own (secret) fault is in ourselves. What kinds of things have you been criticizing someone for behind his or her back? If you were honest with yourself, you would admit you are the one with the real problem, and you are projecting it on someone else.

Developing a positive outlook and happiness in life means you have to think about the best. Positive thinking has to be the first thing -- not the second thing -- or third thing -- on your mind. Thinking about the best is one of the greatest therapies you will find. Train yourself to think about the positive by assessing a fine for each time you have a negative thought. Charge yourself a dollar for each time you catch yourself thinking negatively. (The amount can vary. Just make sure it is enough for it to hurt).

The trap we fall into is the fear of failure. We are so concerned about getting our hopes up too high that we posture ourselves for the worst. This fear is one we have to break through. The only way to be a positive person is to start thinking about positive things. "Positive things" includes our future situations. Think about the best thing happening rather than the worst. Get a big picture of success in your thinking.

Developing a positive outlook and happiness in life means you have to speak only the best about others. What you confess with your voice is how things really are. You can look for the best, think about the best, but unless you confess the best with you mouth, it is not really the truth. The most important thing about this step is you hear yourself say something. When you hear yourself confess something, it removes much doubt in your own mind. Confessing the positive thinking in your own words is life changing. The greatest benefactor to speaking positive is you.

Developing a positive outlook and happiness in life means you have to listen only to the best about others. Steps in developing a positive outlook would not be complete until we address the issue of what you allow yourself to be exposed to. Don't allow yourself to listen to negative things. Do what you have to so that you avoid the negative. Turn off the radio; say good bye and hang up the telephone, tell people to go home for the evening. Just don't sit and take it. Picture negative talk as an air borne disease out to afflict you.

If you shut people off from talking negative around you, they might be offended at first, but their respect for you will grow. Their trust in your integrity will come back to you time and again because they will know they can trust you when they aren't there in person. A positive person has a lot more friends than a negative one!

HAPPINESS COMES AS YOU BEGIN TO THINK POSITIVE. THIS DEVELOPS IN YOUR LIFE BY:

1. Looking only for the best.

2. Thinking only the best.

3. Speaking only the best.

4. Listening only to the best.

DAY 26: LIVE ON/WITH LESS

When you get something new, how long before the new wears off? Usually it is pretty quick. Before long, you wonder why you wanted this thing so bad -- or after the new wears off you are trying to figure out a way to "up grade" the new thing for something even newer.

No matter what you obtain -- an object itself can't bring you any happiness. Happiness comes from the inside, not from the outside, with one exception. This exception has to do with learning to live with less. When it comes to happiness, less is always more.

Living on less money can bring some dimensions of happiness, which have been lost. When you live on less, you will feel more secure about yourself and your future. A sense of destiny will emerge where there was once a sense of fear. This happens because you know that you aren't so dependent on others to survive. Learning to live on less money is always good because it helps us to feel freer to enjoy what life has to offer.

Living on less gives you an emotional/mental edge that people in our culture don't have. As you live on less money, you will become aware of those around you who are totally dependent emotionally/mentally on what they obtain. No longer being dependent what you obtain will put you in a much better position emotionally -- with a much better outlook on life.

Look over how you spend your money. Be honest with yourself: Are there some areas where you are wasting money? Try cutting these areas out completely. The temporary discomfort will be replaced by a joyful sense of inner peace and expansive happiness.

Living with less has the same effect. It seems like we are always plotting, planning, strategizing, and even praying for more "stuff." The more stuff we have, the less happy we become and the less time we have to be happy, since we are spending all our time saving, buying, and worrying about all the extra "stuff" we want!

Learning to live with less means we are going to start saying NO to ourselves. Saying no to yourself helps you get back on track to where you should be. When you are a child you depend on your parent to say NO when you ask for something they think you don't need. When you are an adult, you have to do this yourself. Some of us had a problem in the transition between childhood and adulthood. We never learned to say NO to ourselves when our parents were no longer in the picture. Because we never made the transition between childhood and adulthood well in this way, we are constantly depending on other adults to tell us no. This is too big of a burden on anyone. Each of us is responsible for ourselves. If we have to depend on someone else to tell us no, we are not accepting the responsibility we need to.

Learning to live with less means we are going to have to make do with what we already have. Rather than replace something, try getting it fixed first. Get as much life out of it as possible. Don't give up on it, and you will see that it won't give up on you. Rather than replace something, clean it up. Rarely do we give anything a chance in this way.

Many "things" in our society are made to be disposable. Use it and throw it away. Over the course of time we have become ingrained into this kind of thinking. We even see each other (and relationships) as being disposable, as well.

Learning to live with less means we need to be thankful for what we have and the life we live. Thankfulness does two very important things: 1) it changes up attitudes about how you view something. This new attitude will also affect how you view and treat others. Being thankful for those around you will directly affect how you are treated because a thankful attitude toward others is easily recognized. 2) It helps you become more satisfied with the life you have today. Becoming more satisfied is the most important thing you can do to achieve more happiness in your life. Remember that it is not another "thing" or more "stuff" which can make you happy -- only your thankfulness for what you already have!

LEARNING TO LIVE WITH LESS MEANS YOU:

1. Start saying NO to yourself.

2. Make do with what you have by repairing and cleaning it up.

3. Take some time to be thankful for what you have and the life you live.

DAY 27: ALWAYS BE KIND

No matter how you are treated: BE KIND IN RETURN! It may not be easy, but it pays off in the future like you would never believe.

Kindness is a good habit to gain. There is nothing more positive in life than a person who is kind. People will be attracted to you, they will speak positively about you, and all good things will come to you -- all you need to do is be kind to others.

Kindness is the practical definition of love in a day to day life. There are all kinds of definitions of love, but kindness is the one thing that sums up practical love the best. How do people really know you love them? Only through your attitude and actions toward them. The best display of love is through being kind. Your family, friends, work associates, employees, or employer all deserve the best part of you emotionally. Showing kindness in the face of every kind of circumstance is the one thing that will show everyone that you have love and respect toward them.

Kindness will neutralize situations that have gone too far. The only thing that prevents us from backing down when we know we need to is our selfish pride. Most of the time we need to swallow our pride any way. It doesn't do any good to hold on to your point of view, standing, or attitude. All that does is alienate you from people who could actually help you. Kindness builds up in you the ability to provide the space necessary to resolve important issues. Resolving issues is important in all phases and stages in life. Kindness is a great ally.

Kindness gives you the frame of mind to get rid of guilt. Most of the time when people fuss over issues, everyone feels guilty afterward. No one admits they feel bad, but the surfacing of defensiveness, blame, criticism and other issues show that guilt is present in all parts of a disagreement. If you ever wanted to be the person who didn't feel bad, train yourself to always return kindness, regardless of what people said to you or about you.

Kindness helps you to smile. Smiling is a lost art. Notice people going to and coming from work. Are they smiling? Notice people at work. Are they smiling? Notice people around their homes. Are they smiling? Notice people at the gym, mall or other leisure activities. Are they smiling? We have lost the ability to smile mostly because we have lost touch with simple kindness.

Return kindness for whatever circumstances you face and you will see that happiness in your life will never end.

HAPPINESS IS CREATED BY ALWAYS BEING KIND:

1. Kindness is the practical definition of love.

2. Kindness will neutralize any situation.

3. Kindness gets rid of guilt.

4. Kindness helps you to smile.

DAY 28: LET GO

Letting go does not mean to give up. Letting go has to do with the condition of the will; giving up has to do with the condition of your spirit.

A stubborn will can help defend your inner self from possible potential danger, but most of the time it becomes over-kill. We defend ourselves way too much, and let go way too little. That is why happiness is so elusive. The thing which seems the most unnatural in the face of needing to defend yourself (letting go) is the very thing which can help you with happiness the most.

None of us can go around being defensive about ourselves all the time without it somehow hurting how we view our lives. It robs us of happiness and quality of life to live this way. We need to let go.

We need to let go of things quickly...even as soon as they happen. If you can get yourself to let things go quickly; you are then able to let things just roll off you. Learning to do this as you go will help you not be as sensitive, hurt, or unhappy as before. Don't hold on to what people say to you -- let it go. Don't hold a grudge against something someone did to you -- let it go.

We need to let go of things quietly. One of the reasons we hold on to things for so long, and they trouble us so much, is because we have made such a big deal of them. The louder we are, the longer we hold on. The opposite is also true -- the quieter we are -- the sooner it will be gone. Don't give those things you are holding on to validation by making a big deal about them.

People have a bad habit of trying to vindicate themselves by telling stories to others about how they were treated. Rarely do people you share with feel comfortable telling you the truth. Usually they validate your feelings about what happened. Don't be confused by this kind of validation. If you don't let go of it, you will be the one hurt by it all. It doesn't matter how many people you get who will agree with you -- if you don't let go of it, you will be the one hurt by it. People don't tell you to let go of it and move on with life because they don't want to offend you. What you don't realize is -- they are thinking it!

We need to let go of things daily. We need to take time every single day to ask ourselves -- "What am I holding on to?" "What do I need to let go of?" If we don't do this every day, things, which should not stay with us, usually do.

Asking yourself this strong and direct question will help you to diagnose where you may be carrying things counter to a happy life. Dealing with things as they come is much better than allowing them to mount up.

We need to let go of things consistently. Unless we let go of things consistently, patterns of behavior will become inconsistent. The difficulty is so many people lead inconsistent, unhappy lives and don't even know it. They may know that life is unhappy, but they don't realize there is a better way to live.

Hurt, pain, abuse, and even molestation are things many people carry. Anger, rage, bitterness, resentment and other emotions are the kinds of inner strife people have in their lives. It does not matter how much of a victim you have been in your life; none of it can be taken back. You can't go back and erase bad times. The only thing you can do is let it go.

Happiness can only come to your life if you make room for it. There is only so much energy in the inner life. If you use it up on negative emotions, your inner life will not have the capacity for happiness. The only way to have happiness in your life, is to remove those things in your life which zap the energy that happiness should have. The only way you can make the room, is by making the decision to let go of all those other things that are taking up your time, attention, energy and emotions.

YOUR INNER LIFE IS LIMITED BY YOUR ENERGY. IF YOU ARE GOING TO BE HAPPY YOU ARE GOING TO HAVE TO LET GO OF NEGATIVE THINGS.

1. Let go of things quickly.

2. Let go of things quietly.

3. Let go of things daily.

4. Let go of things consistently.

DAY 29: TAKE A STEP BACK

In the course of life, we often have a tendency to try too hard, get too intense, or work at something too much, to enjoy the fruit of what we are working for. If you are going to enjoy life, you are going to have to take a step back and see things for what they are.

When you are working hard at something, nothing is ever good enough, big enough, or finished enough to be satisfied. It is not until you are deprived or look back later do you realize how good you had it when it was in your hands. By that time, it is often too late to take a step back and start enjoying your life. Doing it now is what happiness is all about.

Ease up...it will help you to take a step back and refocus your attention on what is important. Take time periodically to ease up and look at things a few steps away from the project. Easing up will help you see that there are more important things than just the goals you set that seem like "life or death" at the time.

Ease up every week for a day or two.

Ease up every year for a couple of weeks.

Whether you are easing up every day, every week, or once a year, the step back will have a different kind of meaning to it.

Take a step back and take a look at the bigger picture. The bigger picture is best brought together when you ask yourself why it is you are doing what you are doing.

The why question can really cut to the core of most any project you are working on. When you ask yourself why, you will have done an immediate analysis of the importance of the project. Looking at the bigger picture puts things back into a perspective. It helps makes sense of purpose rather than a position.

Take a step back by creating a memory out of every moment. If you are going to enjoy your life and be happy, memories are a vital part of your existence. Always make it a point to build and create a memory. Do it every day of your life. Enjoy everyone you are with. Allow others to take the time to build a memory. If you go the extra mile in building memories, your life will grow and build in such a positive way; your life will develop a quality beyond your wildest dreams.

Take a step back by squeezing the life out of life. Most people have a tendency to squeeze the life out of others. Instead, you need to squeeze the life out of life. Get the most out of life. Stay active. Keep involved in other people and in other things. Don't let down on life. Enjoy it, and get the most out of it.

Take a step back by not working over time. There are very few people positive about working over time. Workers usually blame the reason for overtime on someone else. The only thing positive gained is the extra money you have the potential to earn. After working overtime for awhile, most people don't see the importance of the money because they are missing out on life. Time with others always creates a greater propensity for happiness than more money. Don't work the over time. Instead, invest that time in others. It will yield you a happier, more satisfying life.

Take a step back by being thankful for your family -- JUST THE WAY THEY ARE. One of the most irritating and frustrating things families try to constantly do is change each other. The reason changing others never works is because people become defensive and untrusting. Defensiveness works counter to changing, and being untrusting works the opposite of being teachable.

You are much better off to simply accept loved ones the way they are, and love them. Love is the best form of nurture. Loving those you love, instead of inspecting them, will build unbreakable bonds of trust between people. Just let love work for you. Your family will be happier, and you will be much happier too!

TAKE A STEP BACK FROM LIFE AND YOU WILL SEE HAPPINESS RETURN TO YOU.

1. Ease up.

2. Look at the big picture.

3. Create a memory out of everything.

4. Squeeze the life out of life.

5. Don't work over time.

6. Love others, rather than just respect them.

DAY 30: LET YOURSELF BE HAPPY

Finally.... and most importantly.... let yourself be happy. You will never be happy until you let yourself. The reason we don't allow ourselves to be happy is because we carry too much unhappiness in our lives that we don't feel worthy to be happy. Because of this, the decision must be made to break out of that kind of attitude and let yourself be happy.

Give yourself permission to be happy. Many times people fall into the pattern of unhappiness because they feel like they don't deserve to be happy. Everyone, no matter what they have done, deserves happiness. If you have been a jerk to others and feel bad about it, make it right. Ask forgiveness, apologize, and pay restitution. Do whatever it takes to remove the load off your shoulders.

Facing up to your failures and mistakes is the biggest part of giving yourself the permission to be happy. Many times people carry this kind of load because they don't think forgiveness is possible. How do you know unless you try? Even if the people you are trying to reach turn you off -- forgive yourself. By doing so, you will have empowered your own life with happiness.

Allow those around you to be happy. An unhappy person rarely lets those around them to be happy. By making the decision to allow those around you to be happy, you will open the door to your own happiness.

When people around you are happy, you will be caught up in their happiness in some way or another. Happiness will not get past you if you allow others to be happy. Seeing others happy will bring happiness immediately upon you. You will see how important happiness is, and will allow yourself to be happy.

Help those around you to be happy. This is especially important if you are having a problem with being happy yourself. If you realize the importance of being happy and that you aren't happy, a fast way to get started is to help others be happy. Encourage others, affirm them, and help them have a pleasant day. This may include helping the atmosphere of the work environment or the feel of your home. It will mean releasing the tension many feel between people, which prevents a feeling of happiness between each other.

In many circles people actually like the tension because it helps with a power and control feeling. As long as this kind of tension is present, happiness will not be. Letting go of the tension in your own feelings will help others let go of their own.

Create happy moments for yourself and others. A happy life is created one moment at a time. These moments are created by one's own choice as life passes by. Take an inventory of yesterday. Ask yourself: Were there some moments I could have enjoyed more? Most likely the answer will be a great big "YES." Learn from it. You can't go back to relive yesterday, but you do have today before you to change this pattern. Create happy moments. Create happy moments when you are on the verge of negative emotions. This way, the happiness will serve to emphasize its importance in your life.

When things in your life are about to go bad -- the decision about how they will turn out is up to you. You can't always change the outcome, but you can always change the way you will view the outcome.

The best way to deal with it is to make the choice to be happy regardless of the outcome of a situation or circumstance. The decision is up to you, not up to the outcome. Life goes on past the moment of the outcome.

Take every opportunity to be happy. This will create a happy life. Life is a series of moments linked together by feelings. If you create moments of happiness and link them with taking every opportunity to be happy, you will be happy. A happy life is the result. LET YOURSELF BE HAPPY!

YOU CAN BE HAPPY IF YOU LET YOURSELF BE HAPPY!

1. Give yourself the permission.

2. Allow those around you to be happy.

3. Help those around you to be happy.

4. Create happy moments.

5. Take every opportunity to be happy.
